The Role of Public Diplomacy in Western Democracies (case study UK 1945 - 2005)

By Barry Vale

Contents

Concluding Remarks

Introduction

Public Diplomacy as a separate concept is only relatively recent, dating back to the 1960s. However, it will be argued that elements of Public Diplomacy have existed, and have therefore been utilised for much longer. Such elements of Public Diplomacy have arguably been used to complement and supplement the more traditional behind the scene diplomacy. This dissertation will also examine the factors that have apparently made Public Diplomacy more visible, if not necessarily more important than traditional forms of diplomacy. The term Public Diplomacy itself was first used by United States government officials from the State Department, whilst academics and the media have increasingly used the term to describe the diplomatic practices and procedures of the Western Democracies. Given the close political, economic, and military links between the United States and the UK there should be no great surprise that both these countries are assumed to use Public Diplomacy as a means of conducting their foreign policy objectives. It could be argued that if used successfully Public Diplomacy allows governments to conduct foreign policy whilst trying to maintain public support for their domestic policies.
Public Diplomacy has strong connections with traditional behind closed doors diplomacy. Governments will use either type of diplomacy in different combinations or singularly depending on the objectives they wish to achieve. Circumstances often dictate the diplomatic measures that all governments of Western Democracies use.

Chapter 1 will discuss how traditional diplomacy developed and how it operated. This chapter will also discuss the origins of Public Diplomacy and whether elements of it are detectable or discernible in past British foreign policy and diplomacy. Traditional British foreign policy has arguably emphasised maintaining the global balance of power, whilst promoting the UK's commercial, territorial, and strategic interests. For instance, attempts to use propaganda or spin to maintain or increase support for wars or unpopular aspects of British foreign policy. It is entirely logical to examine the foreign policy by assessing the main interests of that state and how it can best serve its overriding objectives by interacting with other nation states. The role of non-state organisations and individuals is not always so easy to measure (Barton, 1997 p. 34).

Chapter 2 will focus on the factors that have contributed to the emergence of Public Diplomacy. Therefore, this chapter will examine factors such as the Cold War, the relative economic and military decline of the UK, the emergence of the European integration process, which led to the establishment of the European Union. Finally, changes in the media and altering public attitudes towards the foreign policy of British governments will be examined. Advances in technology have arguably contributed to changes in the way diplomacy is conducted in that governments and non-state organisations have increasingly felt the need to publicise their positions and policy ideas towards general publics and the media. Technological advances have also meant that news and information is spread at a greater speed, increasing the pressure on governments and relevant non-state agencies to act immediately. This chapter will examine the claim of Harold Nicholson amongst others that the international system was altered by the Cold War and led to academic reassessments of how diplomacy operated (Barton, 1997 p. 3).

Chapter 3 will focus on how Public Diplomacy has operated in practice, rather than at a theoretical level. Factors to be examined and assessed will include Public Diplomacy use to counter unpopular foreign policy decisions, as well as its possible manipulation by governments to gain advantage in their diplomatic discussions. Finally, the possible use of Public Diplomacy in complementing and supplementing state diplomacy, such as providing humanitarian relief or specialist services that governments are not in a position to deliver will also be examined. Chapter 3 will also examine how the end of the Cold War and why the expected New World order did not come about, have affected diplomacy (Duffield, 2001 p.1),

Chapter 4 discusses the changes to how diplomacy operates and indeed international relations have been altered by 9/11 and how the various Western Democracies have reacted to the war on terror (Friedman, 2003 p.4). The chapter closes by discussing the future prospects for Public Democracy.

Please note that when appropriate American English spellings have been retained, for instance World Trade Center, and Secretary of Defense.

Please note as the case study is for the sixty year period up to 2005 it will not discuss Brexit. Just how momentous that could be remains to be seen.

Chapter 1

Definitions

Defined in its simplest terms, diplomacy is 'the management of international relations' (Oxford English Reference Dictionary, 1996 p. 401). More specifically diplomacy is a means of one nation state achieving influence over other nation states through negotiation, influence, and persuasion (Baldwin, 1985 p. 13). Therefore, Public Diplomacy is the process of managing or attempting to manage international relations in the public domain, rather than in private behind closed doors traditional diplomacy. The belief that the general public should have any influence over the foreign policy direction and decisions of their own nation states was only mentioned as a possibility towards the end of the 20th century. Decision-making and diplomacy in foreign policy overwhelmingly remains in the hands of national governments, rather than in the hands of their general publics. As will be examined in greater depth later on, although government executives may make the decisions of major national importance and the general public may express its opinion of those decisions, they do not control everything. Rather it is the trained and professional diplomats in combination with technical or legal experts that can have the greatest impact on the implementation of foreign policy decisions. However the expansion of technology and media has influenced the expectations of the public and the attention that governments pay to justifying their policies to domestic and foreign audiences (Evans & Newnham, 1998 p. 453). A recent American report stated that 'Public Diplomacy is the promotion of the national interest by informing, engaging and influencing people around the world' (Djerejian Report, 2003 p. 13).

Public Diplomacy however, is not just diplomacy between nation states; it is diplomacy between individuals, and organisations such as the United Nations and the International Red Cross. The means advocated to achieve Public Diplomacy include cinema, television, radio, popular music, and sport. Such mediums give the opportunity for the peoples, organisations, and governments of different countries to interact with each other through unofficial channels as well as on a formal basis. Public Diplomacy should ideally be used to allow different countries and nationalities to form positive relationships between themselves. However, there is always the potential for Public Diplomacy to be used to propagate or promote one country's culture, moral outlook, or political ideology upon other countries. Whilst definitions of traditional forms of diplomacy have been widely agreed upon defining 'Public Diplomacy' has proved to be difficult and controversial. For instance, although film companies and music producers sell products that collectively could affect the cultures of different countries their main aim is to make profits and not change peoples' ideological or political beliefs. Public diplomacy can also be used to promote academic and research links between countries, for instance Western Democracies agree to assist the education of people from developing states to gain influence upon them whilst the governments of those states hope such links help their national development. Governments on the other hand will always be suspected of acting with ulterior political or economic motives (Wikipedia).

To a certain extent Public Diplomacy could be linked to the process of globalisation, partly because elements of each process have existed for much longer than the terms themselves. Like globalisation, it is a concept that is relatively recent, it can arguably be linked to changes and improvements in technology, and that it can also be argued to show that the decision-making powers of nation states is declining (Nicholson, 2002 p. 12). However, just like globalisation, Public Diplomacy does not have a uniform affect on all nation states, or even on any particular nation. Governments to some extent can control the foreign influences coming into their countries. For example, through strict censorship or import restrictions on foreign made products. France for instance, tried to restrict American films, soft drinks, and companies to protect French culture (and Americans might suggest French profits). Islamic nations can restrict Western imports or ideas as being decadent and contrary to Islamic values. Safety issues can also be used to justify import restrictions, perhaps most famously the banning of British

beef during the 1990s due to the BSE crisis in cattle (Eatwell &
Wright, 2003 p. 161). On the other hand, Public Diplomacy has
been used as a means to project the alleged virtues of liberal
democracies to communist states and also non-western states that
because of their position, history, circumstances, and possibly their
religious beliefs were not willing to adopt Western style democracy
or capitalist economics. The United States is the leading proponent
of promoting its version of liberal democracy, although it will be
argued that the UK has often liked to put forward its own vision of
international relations and attempted to maintain the balance of
power (Morgenthau, 1993 p. 9).

Before the concept of Public Diplomacy was put forward and
developed, diplomacy and foreign policy decision-making and
implementation was the exclusive realm of politicians and
professional career diplomats. Public opinion on foreign policy
issues might have an influence on the conduct of diplomacy, yet it
was national governments that had the final word on what their
countries did in relation to other nation states. Diplomacy was not
for the people to decide upon, their political leaders made the
decisions that either resulted in war or peace, prosperous trade or
impoverished isolation. After making those decisions governments
would then seek to justify the results and consequences of their
diplomatic decisions to their populations if or when they felt there
was a need to do so. Diplomacy was always supposed to be the
main method of ensuring international peace, although it has
sometimes been used to wage war on the most advantageous term
available (Comfort, 1993 p. 158). Studies of diplomacy have
traditionally been state-centric in outlook; in other words largely
adopting the realist approach towards international relations that
maintains nation states are the main components of the global
community. The idealist school that argues that diplomacy should
be conducted on the basis of sound ethics rather than promoting
selfish national interests has had less influence upon governments.
The idealist approach has had a greater impact on non-governmental
organisations that promote humanitarian causes, which frequently
hold ethical viewpoints as opposed to a more overtly political
outlook (Brown, 2001 p. 4).

Diplomacy can, if used sensibly, lead to greater international stability or if used unwisely cannot prevent conflicts. Sometimes wars have deliberately sought such as the three wars Bismarck used to achieve German unification (Hurd, 1997 p. 6). Diplomats and governments may have frequently throughout the centuries publicly proclaimed that they only desire peace yet in private have always sought to achieve their foreign policy goals by any available means. Traditional diplomacy did not always embrace the general public in case such actions would limit the freedom of choice available to national governments. Politicians have not always trusted the opinions of their own general publics, even when they have tried to convince those publics that they are protecting the national interest (Hurd, 1997 p. 7). Governments and diplomats could be argued to have taken Machiavelli's advice to heart as 'one must know how to colour one's actions and to be a great liar and deceiver'. Governments have learnt over the centuries that sometimes the need for deceiving their own populations is on a par with deceiving other countries (Kerr, 1990 p. 80). Diplomacy whether public or behind closed doors is a means of internal and external propaganda as well as communication (Brown, 2001 p. 4).

<u>Diplomacy before Public Diplomacy</u>

The UK alongside older European states such as France has a long history of using traditional behind closed-door diplomacy. Britain for long periods had a very strong position in terms of its diplomatic choices and tactics. Britain was the first country to industrialise, its ready access to usable natural resources and the availability of capital, and abundant trading links were well protected by the Royal Navy. The combination of these factors allowed British governments to bargain or react with other nation states from a position of strength (Hobsbawm, 1962 p. 38). Such was the extent of Britain's commercial and naval prowess that the term 'gunboat diplomacy' was used to describe the practice of British governments of sending Royal Navy ships to trouble spots. British warships were sent to fly the flag, whilst the possibility that they would turn their guns on other nation states would frequently convince other governments that it was a wise option to do whatever the British government wanted them to do (Comfort, 1993 p. 158). The period after the Napoleonic Wars to the First World War has frequently been termed the 'Pax Britannica' because Britain was the strongest power in the world. During this period British governments did not have to resort to Public Diplomacy, they also had the option to stay out of conflicts or to intervene whenever they wanted to do so. Economic and naval strength meant Britain remained at peace except for the Crimean War and various colonial conquests and campaigns, most notably the Boer War in South Africa. The saying that the sun never set upon the British Empire was a boast based on fact (Evans & Newnham, 1998 p.422). The Boer War was not fought as a result of Public Diplomacy; it was fought to end Boer moves towards independence. Despite opposition from the Liberal Party, the Boer War was generally popular with the British public who wanted to avenge the early defeats of the British Army. That conflict led to reforms of the structure and training of the British Army that paid dividends during the First World War. Once the Boer War was won the Prime Minister, Lord Salisbury found it as electorally favourable as Margaret Thatcher found the victory in the Falklands War eighty years later. Patriotism can be a vital part of any government gaining domestic support for its foreign policy, especially if that involves fighting wars (Comfort, 1993 p. 54). Propaganda to justify wars and maximise internal support combined with foreign acceptance of foreign policy is a main theme of Public Diplomacy with a long tradition that easily predates the use of the actual term Public Diplomacy (Hurd, 1997 p.6). The world's strongest powers have generally felt that it was important to have a positive image of their foreign policy and diplomacy in other countries as means to maintain or even to improve their international position and prestige (Evans & Newnham, 1998 p. 422).

The First World War would effectively end the era of the Pax Britannica. Although, it was still possible to argue that Britain was the dominant global power until the Second World War, the international perceptions of British power and influence altered which affected the effectiveness of the UK's diplomacy. In economic terms, the United States and Germany overtook Britain around 1900. It was German attempts at ending the Royal Navy's naval supremacy that contributed most towards the worsening relations between Britain and Germany. British diplomacy even entered into tentative understandings with France and to a lesser extent Russia that fell short of a full alliance, whilst attempting to counter the growing German threat. It was German ambition rather than British or French diplomacy that did much to start the First World War (Hurd, 1997 p. 38). There was popular support in Britain for ensuring that the Royal Navy retained its numerical and qualitative superiority over the German Navy, even if there were doubts about establishing strong links with France. The First World War was of course caused by events in the Balkans, rather than by a direct conflict between Britain and Germany. The Germans breaching Belgian neutrality in order to attack France triggered British entry into the First World War. The declaration of war was initially very popular with the British public, as it was with the populations of the other countries that became involved. The British government had to increase its use of internal propaganda and diplomatic efforts to increase international support once it became apparent that the war would not a short one (Roberts, 1996 pp. 446-47).

The diplomatic consequences of the First World War were as profound as the political, military, economic, and strategic consequences of that terrible conflict. The scope and duration of the war severely damaged the economic, military, and human resources of Britain and its Empire. The devastation of the First World War brought dramatic consequences across Europe, to France, Germany, to the successor states to Austria-Hungary, and Russia in particular (James, 2003 p. 2). The First World War meant British governments gained experience of being in an alliance with France and Russia; with the United States becoming an ally as well by the end of the war. British diplomacy and its intelligence services had been particularly effective in persuading the United States to join the war on the allied side (Ward, 2003 p. 238). The leaking of the Zimmerman Telegram (which detailed German attempts to get Mexico to attack the United States) and the German use of unrestricted submarine warfare brought the Americans into the war and meant that Britain was on the winning side (Hobsbawm, 1994 p.28).

The Treaty of Versailles, the American reversion into isolation, combined with the weakened status of Germany and revolutionary Russia meant that Britain held its position as a great power during the Inter-War period. However, the founding of the League of Nations increased the scope for Public Diplomacy, as there was a non-governmental organisation that had diplomatic objectives of its own. Rebuilding war torn Europe and supporting homeless and stateless refugees through the auspices of the International Red Cross also gave an opportunity for diplomacy at a non-state level (Brendon, 2000 p. 15). The British influence at Versailles was not as strong as might have been expected, the French had the strongest influence, which meant the final settlement was harsh towards Germany and an underlying cause of future conflict. An increasing reluctance to get involved in fighting conflicts showed that Britain was suffering from war weariness, as well as economic weaknesses (Roberts, 1996 p. 456). British governments faced greater strains on their resources due to American unwillingness to become involved in world politics outside the immediate areas of American interest, which did not include sorting out European squabbles. It did not involve joining the League of Nations even though it had been the idea of President Woodrow Wilson. The existence of the League of Nations meant that there was an extra area for British diplomacy to operate within, it also increased opportunities for the publicising of foreign issues. At another level it allowed British citizens join an organisation that aimed to promote global security even though it lacked the resources to do so (Ryan, 2003 p. 19).

Perhaps the Inter-war period was unusual in that the foreign policy objectives of successive British governments and the mood of the British public largely coincided as they all wished to avoid war. British governments were keen to publicly announce their desire for peace and stability. The Anglo-Irish War ended in bloody stalemate, the British could not regain Southern Ireland, whilst the Irish Republicans could not gain control of six of the Ulster counties. Compromise in the form of partition was reached because the British government no longer wanted to fight. Whilst the Irish Republican Army (IRA) and Sinn Fein did not want to find out if Lloyd George was bluffing about using the Royal Navy to shell Dublin if they did not sign a peace treaty (Schama, 2002 p. 443). Severe financial constraints and an unwillingness to repeat the slaughter of the

Western Front meant that British governments made the avoidance of conflicts the overriding aim of British diplomacy. Amongst the British public the jingoism of the Boer War and August 1914 was replaced by a strong aversion to war, embodied in the phrase 'never again' (Morgan, 1993 p. 598). The burden of the British Empire actually increased after the First World War with the acquisition of Iraq and Palestine as mandated territories run on behalf of the League of Nations. At this juncture neither British governments nor the British public was willing to end the British Empire (Hobsbawm, 1994 p. 38). Limitations to British naval power were demonstrated by Britain's inability to keep pace in the emerging naval arms race between itself, the United States, and Japan. In contrast to the pre-war naval arms race with Germany, the British government stuck to its financial limits. British diplomacy was prominent in halting the naval arms race through the Washington Naval Treaty. Britain agreed to build new battleships at the same ratio as the Americans and only two more than Japan. This effectively meant the British had accepted that the United States Navy would become the world's largest navy. The brand new battlecruiser HMS Hood would be used to fly the flag, yet would not be joined by large numbers of more powerful capital ships (Johnston & McAuley, 2000 p. 113).

During the inter-war period collective security in the form of the League of Nations was hoped to be the best means of resolving international disputes before they escalated into wars and violence. When it suited British governments they would use the League of Nations as part of their diplomatic strategies, when it did not suit them British governments would act unilaterally, or act in unison with other powers, most notably France. Whilst the British public and governments might have hoped that the League of Nations would prevent another global conflict, the League was with hindsight destined to failure from the outset. The League was weakened without the United States and the Soviet Union as members and with Germany initially excluded, the League of Nations lacked military strength and just as importantly political and diplomatic credibility. British governments saw the League as an extra dimension to their diplomacy; it increased their scope to act publicly rather than behind closed doors (Hurd, 1997 p. 62). Although the League settled some minor disputes during the 1920s, it was unable to deal with the aggressive acts of Germany, Italy, and Japan during the 1930s. Arguably, British governments contributed to that failure by not being prepared to take military action, or allow for economic sanctions to be applied effectively against such aggressor states. British diplomacy was not a great success story, although British governments believed they maintained public support because war was avoided. In the end war was not avoided it was only delayed (Hurd, 1997 p. 62). Successive Prime Ministers especially Neville Chamberlain did not believe that the Axis powers in general and Germany in particular wanted another world conflict (Middlemas, 1972 p. 116). Throughout much of the inter-war period British diplomacy was seriously constrained by a knowledge of the country's economic weakness and an obsessive fear of the revolutionary threat posed by the Soviet Union. The lack of military capabilities meant that the Axis powers were not deterred by British diplomacy. The inability to work with the Soviet Union further undermined collective security (Brendon, 2000 p. 53).

The Great Depression, which greatly assisted Adolf Hitler's rise to power in Germany also, had consequences for the conduct of British diplomacy during the 1930s. Defence spending had already been greatly reduced during the 1920s, ironically enough when Winston Churchill was Chancellor of the Exchequer and before he became the most vocal opponent of appeasement. When faced with the Great Depression the Labour government and later the National government introduced austerity measures to balance the national budget. Further cutting the defence budget and rather more controversially at the time, by cutting unemployment benefits saved public money and balanced the budget. Such disarmament would not have had as much diplomatic impact if it had not coincided with the emergence of Germany, Japan, and to a lesser extent Italy as military threats to international peace and British national interests. The Great Depression distracted British governments with domestic social, economic, and political problems. At the same time it lessened their capabilities of dealing with an increasingly hostile diplomatic and international set of situations. The knowledge of the UK's weak economic, military, and naval positions increased the inclination of governments towards appeasement. The Munich Agreement was at the time considered to be a diplomatic success, although Neville Chamberlain's pledge of 'peace in our time' was proved to be naïve. The British government portrayed that agreement as needed to prevent war; a position that most of the public accepted until Germany occupied the remnants of Czechoslovakia in 1939 (James, 2003 p. 123).

The Impact of the Second World War

During the 1930s the British public had no control over British foreign policy, like their government they may have wished to avoid war, yet they had no control over events. Instead of resisting aggression British diplomacy sought to appease or simply ignore acts of aggression. The government assumed that the British public did not particularly care about what the Japanese did in Manchuria, what the Italians did in Ethiopia, or for that matter what the Germans did to Austria and Czechoslovakia. There was only public disquiet in Britain once it emerged that the British government had all but given Mussolini a free hand in Ethiopia, despite publicly stating its support for collective security and economic sanctions (Brendon, 2000 p. 271). In 1936 the Royal Navy still had enough power to sink or blockade any Italian ship that was destined for Ethiopia, as Winston Churchill for one said it should be allowed to do. Neither the British nor the French used their joint control of the Suez Canal to stop Italian ships using it (Kennedy, 1976 p. 289). However, no military or naval action was taken at all to stop the Italian invasion, even though they used poison gas. Military action was not taken to prevent Italy joining an alliance with Germany. However, the ineffective economic sanctions that the League of Nations applied did nothing to save Ethiopia and merely ensured an alliance between Italy and Germany (Hobsbawm, 1994 p. 37). The Nazi regime, it could be argued, used elements of Public Diplomacy to promote itself to foreign audiences. Hitler had a gift for propaganda and the ability to conceal his real motives. The Nazi regime had successfully presented itself as being responsible for German economic recovery and a return to great power status. The Nuremberg rallies as well as the autobahns, and the Berlin Olympics symbolised Germany's renewed sense of purpose. It seems that Hitler had an astuteness for successfully using the main elements of Public Diplomacy that left all British politicians apart from Winston

Churchill looking like clueless amateurs (Hobsbawm, 1994 p 38).

The Second World War would affect British diplomacy more profoundly than any previous other conflict. The relationship with France became very strained due to the French being defeated in 1940, whilst Britain fought on alone. Her survival chances were doubted by many other countries, although Winston Churchill was able to revive domestic and international confidence that Britain would do just that. Hitler felt safe enough from the threat of Britain being able to liberate Western Europe from German control, that he launched the invasion of the Soviet Union. The Second World War witnessed the alliance between the Soviet Union, the United States and Britain. Britain was very much the junior partner; the United States would provide most of the military equipment and finance, with the Red Army having to do the bulk of the fighting. Although Winston Churchill rightly regarded Nazi Germany as the main enemy, it was the war in the Far East that had the greatest consequences for the British Empire. Japan rapidly conquered the British colonies of Burma, Malaya, Hong Kong, and Singapore. The fall of Singapore was Britain's most humiliating military defeat. The over-stretched Royal Navy was unable to save the day and took heavy loses, the garrison was very badly led and surrendered without much of a fight. The Japanese even threatened India before the tide was turned. The experience of Japanese occupation would increase demands for independence from all the colonies involved except for Hong Kong. In India the perilous nature of Britain's declining power did not go unnoticed. Overall the cost of fighting the Second World War was high, and would have been even higher without the Lend- Lease programme (Stafford, 1999 p. 62).

Chapter 2

Post-war Diplomatic and Political developments

As the previous chapter amply demonstrated there had been little scope for Public Diplomacy before the end of the Second World War. The consequences of the Second World War were even greater than those of the First World War had been, with British power eclipsed by the United States and the Soviet Union. There were great changes to the international system that alongside technological and economic changes that increased the scope for Public Diplomacy. With the exception of the United States and Canada, the Western Democracies had been badly affected by the war. France, the Low Countries, Denmark, and Norway had to recover from the effects of German occupation and fighting. Germany and Italy had been devastated in defeat with Germany partitioned under allied control. The territorial boundaries of post-war Europe were decided by the United States, the Soviet Union and Britain at the Yalta and Potsdam conferences. These conferences were carried out in secret until decisions had already been made. The British and Americans had publicly expressed their desire to bring liberal democracy to all of Europe, although that was contradicted by allowing the Soviets to dominate Central and Eastern Europe. From a realist perspective it would have been impossible to stop that domination. The end of the war also saw the formation of the UN, which was intended to ensure peace and security (Kissinger, 1994, p.435). Although on the winning side, Britain had to face up to the cost of post-war reconstruction and the cost of paying for the war, whilst trying to maintain as much of the British Empire as possible, or carrying out de-colonisation with the minimal amount of conflict. However, immediate post-war circumstances and the election of the first Labour government with an overall majority meant realignments in British foreign policy. These changes inadvertently led to more chances for Public Diplomacy. Post-war governments found it difficult to balance the reality of British weakness with the belief that the UK remained a great power. The increased use of Public Diplomacy can be partially attributed to these governments attempting to hide or even reverse the UK's declining global position. Public Diplomacy can be a cover for weakness as well as an excuse for aggression or indeed inaction when governments are faced with international problems (Nicholson, 2002, p.101).

Ideologically, the Labour government elected in 1945 was committed to shrinking the British Empire. The financial strains of the Second World War gave a cost cutting imperative to de-colonisation. Britain could no longer afford the cost of maintaining its army in India, where an increasing number of its people wanted independence. Neither did the Labour government wish to keep the army stationed in Palestine, where it was caught between the violence of the Arab-Israeli conflict. Ending British rule in India removed the largest colony from the British Empire and increased arguments about ending direct British rule of all colonies east of the Suez Canal. The de-colonisation process would prove to be complicated by the onset of the Cold War and the desire of British governments to contain the spread of communism in its colonies before granting independence. Amongst its colonies in Africa, the British governments did not believe that all the colonies were economically and politically developed enough for independence. There was no role for Public Diplomacy in the course of giving India independence, although the government presented the granting of independence as the best option for ensuring peace and stability (Nicholson, 2002 p.87). British foreign policy was intended to only give independence to colonies if the subsequent independent regimes were pro-British in policy and were not communist or socialist in outlook. The independence of Kenya and Malaya was delayed until power could be given to governments that did not risk or endanger British commercial and political interests. The violent and non-violent counter-insurgency tactics used in Kenya and Malaya were later adopted less successfully by the United Sates in Vietnam. The British government was fortunate that the earlier conflicts received much less media coverage than American involvement in Vietnam (Curtis, 2004).

A by-product of the de-colonisation process was the issue of immigration, which was also linked to a policy of using immigrant workers to relieve the post-war labour shortages. Post-war immigration would not only help diversify British society, it would also influence Public Diplomacy in Britain as there are now parts of British society that are concerned about developments in Asia, Africa and the West Indies. Immigrants and their descendants would want the British government to treats its former colonies favourably, and to intervene during humanitarian crisis's or to end or prevent conflict. The Foreign Office also sought to maintain friendly relationships with former colonies to promote British trade and the economic and political development within the former colonies. UK governments have viewed the Commonwealth as a means to exert diplomatic influence (Evans & Newnham, 1998 p.242). Immigration would have a wide political, cultural, social, and economic impact on the UK. Despite racism and discrimination non-white immigrants remained in Britain. These immigrants and their families have enriched the country's culture and have increased Britain's links to other countries. Electorally ethnic minority groups have been important, especially in marginal inner city constituencies, their votes were particularly important to the Labour Party. These groups tended to believe that Labour carried out domestic and foreign policies that helped them more than the Conservatives, who did not attempt to gain their votes or support (Comfort, 1993 p. 498). Although most of the immigrants moved to working class areas and did manual jobs, some Asians were able to do white collar and professional jobs. Non-white immigration meant that UK had to consider race relations and about relations with ethnic communities. Governments would have to consider changing its diplomatic relations with countries that been the homelands of immigrants (Schama, 2002 p.552). Non-white immigrants and their families have also brought different religions to Britain including Islam, Hinduism, and the Sikh religion. Muslims in particular regard their religion as being a global community and tend to take great interest in foreign events, which affect Muslims. That concern increases the possibility that Muslims would wish to influence the UK's diplomacy on issues they believed could have an impact upon the global Islamic community (Abercrombie, Turner & Hill, 2000 p.49).

The need for post-war reconstruction and the event of the Cold War meant British diplomacy had to adapt to very different circumstances. The United Nations (UN) replaced the League of

Nations, with the United States and the Soviet Union joining from the beginning, although it may not have become as effective as some hoped, it has proved more enduring than the League of Nations. Britain was given the prestigious position of being a permanent member of the UN Security Council. The UN has bodies such as UNICEF that aim to improve the lives of certain groups, such as children and refugees. Public Diplomacy can therefore have the role of increasing public awareness and support for the UN and it's various projects and programmes, all sometimes UK governments have been prepared to diplomacy and to publicly communicate its ignoring or differing interpretations of UN resolutions (Morgenthau, 1993 p.120). The existence of such bodies allows non-governmental organisations the opportunity to participate in Public Diplomacy, they have access to media resources that the majority of individuals lack or are unable to use. The post-war British governments have all claimed to be strong supporters of the UN, helping to ensure collective security and protect countries that were attacked or violated by stronger states. Just like the other four permanent members of the Security Council. British enthusiasm for the UN and when it has defended the defenceless was selective and depended upon who needed to be protected. This was particularly true during the Cold War. Governments have used the media to justify their reasons for intervention or non-interventions when it comes to supporting the UN. Governments have a long track record of upholding British national interests ahead of ethically based decision-making, a trait that it has in common with the majority of nation states. Public Diplomacy came into its own when UK governments took unethical decisions as part of the Cold War struggle between east and west (Curtis, 2004).

The United States is in the best position to use Public Diplomacy as a means to spread its version of events across the globe. This is due to American television channels, films, popular music, and other consumer products being amongst the most influential and recognisable brands in the world. American governments are well aware of such influences, and have tried to use those influences for diplomatic, economic, and political gains over the past several decades. A common language, strong cultural, economic, and political links means the UK can be influenced by events and developments across the Atlantic. Of course, UK governments have not been, and are not averse to using the same methods or techniques, even if they cannot match the scale or the budget of American Public Diplomacy operations. Public Diplomacy is a means of communicating with other countries and developing relationships with them. However the UK has retained the ability to have a strong cultural influence upon other countries particularly English speaking ones. British governments have a high capacity to mobilise public opinion domestically and abroad that is probably only surpassed by the American government (Chossudovsky, 3 February 2003).

The Cold War and its influence

There was a fear that communism would spread across Western Europe if proactive measures had not been taken to avoid it. Although Stalin had promised at Yalta and Potsdam not to take Soviet forces further west than the Soviet occupation zone in Germany. There were some doubts in the West as to how far Stalin could be trusted. The use of the media to present liberal democracy as the best means of ensuring peace, stability, and prosperity was part of the proactive measures to prevent the spread of communism and to justify the Western stance during the Cold War (Todd, 2001 p.115). Communist parties were strongly supported in France and Italy, although efforts were made to keep them out of coalition governments. The efforts of the Greek communists to seize power had resulted in civil war with the Greek government supported by Britain. Fear of the spread of communism led to the decision by the UK, the United States, and France to rebuild the West German economy which had been completely destroyed through bombing and fighting. The UK had wanted West German economic reconstruction to drive forward economic growth in Western Europe, although the French had wanted to stop Western Germany becoming economically powerful again. In the end France supported West German economic growth, as that growth was contained and guided within the process of European integration (McCormick, 2002 p.10).

The British government was keener on establishing close military links with the rest of Western Europe and also in finding ways of keeping an American military presence in Western Europe. The worsening relationship between the Soviet Union and the United States, which resulted in the Cold War, meant that the Americans kept a much larger military presence in Western Europe than originally intended, which would have been just enough personnel to secure the American occupation zones of Germany and Austria. However, as the Soviet Union managed to turn all the states of Central and Eastern Europe into ones controlled by communist regimes President Truman decided to maintain significant levels of American military forces in Western Europe (Todd, 2001 p. 117). Given the superior numbers of Soviet conventional weapons and the greater size of the Soviet Army, it was not surprising that the UK and the other Western European wanted* as well as needed the Americans to defend them. Britain and others did not wish to get caught behind what Winston Churchill described as the 'iron curtain' (Resources for the Study of International Relations and Foreign Policy).

Building formal military alliances did not take too long with the onset of the Cold War. Stalin's attempt to blockade West Berlin had been broken by the efforts of the USAF, the RAF, and countless civilian pilots in the Berlin Airlift that contributed to rising tensions between East and West. Such events led to the formation of the North Atlantic Treaty Organisation (NATO) in 1949. NATO formally ensured that the Americans would remain involved in defending Western Europe for as long as there remained a threat from the Soviet Union and its allies. The establishment of NATO also explicitly offered all its Western European members American nuclear protection once the Soviet Union had successfully developed its own nuclear weapons. Both countries having nuclear capabilities further enhanced their position as superpowers (Evans & Newnham, 1998 p. 72). Despite being satisfied with the foundation of NATO, the post-war Labour government decided to develop British atomic bombs. That decision was made as much for reasons of prestige as for sound or logical defence and foreign policy considerations. The development of a British nuclear deterrent combined with the decision to allow the Americans to base their nuclear weapons in the UK would both prove controversial and invoke opposition from the

1950s (Clarke, 2005 p.14). The Atlee government took the decision to develop the atomic bomb to give the UK greater freedom of movement in diplomacy in relation to the United States as much as the Soviet Union. Foreign Secretary Ernest Bevin argued that if the UK had nuclear weapons it might stop the Americans dictating to the British government, as it had done over war debts and ending the Empire (Bullock, 1983 p. 352). In practical terms the independence of the UK's independent nuclear deterrent has to be questioned, as it would not be used without the prior agreement of the Americans. The UK has frequently had to rely on American technology and weapons to maintain its nuclear forces (Greenwood, 2000 p. 109). The UK has often had to play a supportive role to American foreign policy objectives, which had the side effect of limiting Public Diplomacy, a good example was allowing the Americans to base cruse missiles in the UK (Spiller Et al, 2005 p.295). The UK believed that gaining such nuclear technology was a benefit of its special relationship with the United States (Young, 2003 p. 127).

In the early 1950s much of British diplomacy was diverted towards allowing West Germany to re-arm. Other Western European states, France in particular, did not want West German re-armament. The concept of the European Defence Community (EDC) was put forward as a compromise to allow it under controlled circumstances. Although the French government agreed to the EDC, the French National Assembly never ratified it. In the end West Germany re-armed under the auspices of NATO with the provision that West German forces never operated outside of NATO areas (Dunbabin, 1994 p. 100). The UK was in agreement with The West German government that Western Europe was stronger economically and militarily with a strong West Germany (Bark & Gress, 1993 p. 252).

Membership of NATO meant that Britain had more effective defence and foreign policies without reducing any of its national sovereignty. Being able to retain full sovereignty was part of the attraction of that organisation. Developing a British nuclear deterrent was done to give the country extra status, although it had not always been significant in comparison to the number of nuclear weapons held by the Soviet Union and the United States. Since the early 1960s British governments have been part of attempts to prevent nuclear proliferation, signing the nuclear non-proliferation treaty in 1968 (Brown with Ainley, 2005 p. 110). There were protests about Britain having nuclear weapons, most notably amongst those organisations by the Campaign for Nuclear Disarmament (CND). Although such protests were highly vocal and received a great deal of media coverage, these protests made no discernible difference to British foreign policies. Besides both the Labour and Conservative parties were committed to Britain retaining its nuclear power status and only envisaged nuclear disarmament through multilateral agreements, rather than unilateral action. Indeed, when the Labour party endorsed unilateral disarmament during the early 1980s, it greatly contributed to its electoral decline (Coxall, Leach, & Robbins 2003 p.200).

British diplomacy and European Integration

The task of economic reconstruction in Western Europe provided a rational argument for developing the process of European integration, which although British governments supported, they did not initially join in as they believed maintaining links with the British Empire and the Commonwealth as more important. There was also the belief that the special relationship with the United States was even more important. Britain was in serious financial difficulties once the Americans ended the lend-lease programme, forcing the domestic rationing of bread and the decision to withdraw British forces from Greece. The British government announcement that it could no longer support the Greek government in the Greek civil war prompted the United States government to develop Marshall Aid to finance the re-construction of Western Europe. Marshall Aid proved instrumental in reviving the economies of Western Europe in general and West Germany in particular. Britain was to stay out of the European Coal and Steel Community (ECSC), which later became the European Economic Community (EEC) and is now the European Union (EU). Belatedly, Britain would form the European Free Trade Association to improve its trading links with Western Europe before attempting to join the EEC (Watson, 1997 p.

129). British governments changed their opinion about joining the EEC, as the stronger economic growth of the original six members became apparent. The two main obstacles to British membership were the opposition of President de Gaulle and lack of enthusiasm of the British public (James, 2003 p. 271). British governments also believed that EEC membership would not prove to be a hindrance to the special relationship with the United States, which did not always seem special, especially after the Suez crisis of 1956. Sometimes the relationship between London and Washington seemed based on necessity rather than affection. Harold Macmillan as Prime Minister felt that the relationship suffered as a result of the American sense of superiority (Horne, 1989 p.208).

British diplomacy and its nature were altered by its eventually joining the EEC. Being a member of EFTA had not been as economically beneficial as anticipated. Britain's economic growth rates were lower than those experienced by the six original members of the EEC. Unfortunately for the British governments of the 1960's, General de Gaulle of France vetoed their applications to join the EEC (Eatwell & Wright, 2003 p.160). The issue of joining the EEC caused much debate and divided the Conservative and Labour parties. As Prime Minister Edward Heath would take the UK into the EEC only with the help of Labour MPs such as Roy Jenkins who defied the party whip to vote in favour of memberships. Opponents of Britain's entry included the Conservative MP Enoch Powell as well as Labour left wing MPs, such as Tony Benn and Michael Foot (Benn, 1988 p.313). Opponents of UK membership argued that the EEC would drastically reduce the UK's sovereignty. Unluckily enough for Edward Heath, Britain's entry into the EEC coincided with poor economic growth, higher inflation and increasing unemployment, a situation made worse by the Oil Crisis of 1973. That crisis underlined the dependence of the UK upon Middle East oil supplies (Evans & Newnham, 1998 p. 399). The Conservatives lost power in February 1974 and the incoming Wilson government was deeply divided as to whether Britain should remain in the EEC or leave. Wilson restored Labour party unity by holding a referendum on the issue (Gowland & Turner, 2000 p.130). The result was a clear yes for remaining within the EEC, yet it was hardly an enthusiastic endorsement. At this point Labour was more opposed to the EEC than the Conservatives. By the time of the 1983 general election Labour advocated that the UK should leave the EEC, which again contributed to its dismal share of the popular vote (Coxall, Robins, & Leach, 2003 p. 2000).

The opportunities for Public Diplomacy increased in the UK for various reasons in the post-war period. Increasing availability of information about the situations in other countries played a part in these developments. Firstly, news of foreign events reached the UK more rapidly due to radio broadcasts improved newspaper coverage and the development of television services. Even if newspapers, radio and television broadcasts were not critical of the UK governments' foreign policy decisions and actions, they were providing greater levels of information about what the government did and why it did it. Television gave the impression that the world was getting smaller, as more people could afford to have sets; more people were able to see more global events unfold in their living rooms. Before the use of televisions became widespread people had only been able to watch news footage at cinema, sometimes days after events had actually happened. It is not surprising that Public Diplomacy was formally developed in the United States, as this is where the expansion of media coverage happened first and at the fastest rate. American governments portrayed themselves as the protectors of Western Democracies and of capitalism in the struggle against communism and the Soviet Union. Whilst they could justify interventions, such as backing South Korea in the Korean War (Ryan, 2003 p. 62). Britain's status as a great power, as well as it is economic stability was to be assured by working closely with the Americans. UK governments had tried to influence American foreign policy when it has suited for interests to do so. For instance, in 1953 the British and Americans worked together to overthrow the Iranian government to prevent the nationalisation of the oil industry in Iran (Curtis, 2004). Other interventions in Latin America and Asia were morally more dubious and were potentially more contentious. Public Diplomacy was supposedly developed to allow the public greater influence over diplomacy, yet it also increases the opportunity for governments to present their side to every issue or event, truth, propaganda, or spin depending on an individual's opinion. In other words, Public Diplomacy can be as much about manipulating media coverage and public opinion as it is about affecting foreign policy decisions. British governments are aware that their foreign policy decisions can harm their reputations if they are believed to fail, although usually it is the success or failure of their domestic policies that determine their electoral fate. At any rate most Prime Ministers concentrate on domestic affairs unless circumstances give their foreign policy or diplomacy greater prominence (Young, 2003 p. 321).

Another factor in the increase in those that wished to develop Public Diplomacy is related to improved levels of education and higher living standards. Previously, the people most influencing foreign policy and diplomacy were usually connected to businesses hoping for good relationships with other countries to maintain or improve trading links. Aside from defence manufacturers, humanitarian organisations were also interested in how diplomacy operated, although for different motivations. Such groups and organisations have attempted to lobby or provide information to governments in order to influence foreign policy decisions. Higher education standards and better living standards acted as a catalyst for the formations of interest groups such as Amnesty International, CND and Friends of the Earth that wished to influence diplomacy and other related areas of government policy such as defence or environmental policy. These groups wanted to change government policies and believe that gaining public support is the best means of persuading governments to do what they want them to do. The emergence of pressure groups provides governments with an incentive to promote and defend their policy decisions through the media and television coverage. The existence of pressure groups justifies the use of government press offices and Public Diplomacy (Madgwick, 1994 p. 345). Governments have adopted the use of press offices and Public Diplomacy on a full time basis as their critics and pressure groups constantly seek to change public opinion, rather than just during election campaigns (Barry, 2000 p.302).

Chapter 3

<u>The Thatcher Effect</u>

As discussed in the previous chapter Public Diplomacy can be argued to have increased in scope, and size, although it is debatable as to whether it has become influential upon foreign policy decision-making in the UK. The changes in media coverage, and just as importantly a more critical attitude towards governments have altered the cultural, political, and economic landscape with a knock on affect on the conduct of diplomacy (Curtis, 2004). Reputations and political careers can be made and broken with greater speed than witnessed previously. The consequences of one country's actions, or the actions of individuals and organisations can be broadcast and assessed globally within seconds. To a certain extent image has become more important than substance in the carrying out of diplomacy. Politicians, individuals, and organisations are often vying with each other to gain media coverage. The digital age is an age in which headline-catching sound bites are deemed a greater priority than the formation and implementation of coherent policies or diplomacy. Greater media coverage is both a cause and affect of the need for Public Diplomacy to promote and justify the diplomacy of UK governments (Gott, 2005). The UK, like other Western Democracies, is usually in a position were the government and various interested groups are competing with soap operas, popular music, and sports events to receive television and media coverage. That is not to say that governments do not try to influence the media coverage they receive, interference that is in their view justified due to times of diplomatic tensions, and in wartime conditions. Often the issues relating to foreign policy issues and decisions are complex; Governments tend to simplify those issues in order to present their decisions in the most favourable light. British governments are not unusual in having used elements of Public Diplomacy to further their arguments, particularly when they are uncertain about the popularity of their policies. Public Diplomacy is more likely to be used when governments are unsure of their popularity at home and anxious to maintain Britain's status abroad (ePilitix.com).

The effectiveness of the Public Diplomacy used by UK governments or those that have wished to influence them depends on circumstances, and how convincingly arguments have been put forward. The support of the general public tends to fluctuate from issue to issue, yet can also depend upon the popularity of the governing party in domestic issues (Gott, 2005). For instance, Margaret Thatcher was not particularly popular at the start of her first term, due especially to the worst post-war economic recession and rising unemployment. However, her intransigence towards the other EEC governments over the issue of the UK receiving a budgetary rebate, which earned her the plaudits of right wing newspapers and those members of the public sceptical about British membership. Margaret Thatcher was also an unstinting backer of Ronald Reagan's tough stance against the Soviet Union as superpower relations worsened, living up to her nickname of the Iron Lady (Coxall, Robins, & Leach, 2003 p.200). It was an unexpected event that salvaged her first term in office, the Falklands War, and showed her ability to gain favourable media coverage as well as diplomatic support. Argentina invaded the Falkland Islands in April 1982, quickly overwhelming the tiny British garrison based there. The Argentine military junta expected and gambled upon a quick victory to maintain its hold on power. Instead Margaret Thatcher was determined to regain the Falkland Islands by force if needs be. Her decision to send a Royal Navy task force was popular with the general public, as was her determination to not let Britain remain humiliated. Initially, the United States and other Western European countries urged a peaceful solution to the crisis. Fortunately for Margaret Thatcher, Ronald Reagan believed that America's relationship with the UK was more important than its links with Argentina. Whilst Secretary of State Alexander Haig was trying to broker a peaceful solution, Secretary of Defense, Casper Weinberger had already allowed weapon supplies to the British task force. The UK government was able to gain favourable domestic and international support as it was resisting aggression from another state that had an undemocratic military government. Domestically little had to be done to gain popular support for retaking the Falklands (Dickie, 1994 p. 181). Any lingering hopes for a peaceful solution were ended when a Royal Navy submarine sank the Argentine cruiser the General Belgrano in controversial circumstances. The British had unilaterally placed a 200 mile exclusion zone around the Falkland Islands, there was much debate as to whether the General Belgrano was inside that zone, and in which way the ship had been sailing. British attempts at propaganda might have been more effective if the then Defence Secretary John Knot had given more consistent accounts (Kerr, 1990 p. 480). Despite the loss of several ships the Royal Navy was able to land British forces on the Falkland Islands. Once ashore the superior training and quality of British forces soon defeated the Argentine forces. Victory in the Falklands War boosted the popularity of the Thatcher government, or more accurately decreased its unpopularity. The Falklands factor was widely credited for the Conservative election victory in 1983, although the divisions and left ward lurch of the Labour Party was also important. For the Thatcher government it represented a victory that enhanced the Prime Minister's reputation for being a woman that got results. Aside from the sinking of the General Belgrano the government's managing of the media had been astute, whilst internationally it showed that the UK was not a weak country in decline (Coxall, Robins, & Leach, 2003 p.200).

Margaret Thatcher gained a reputation of being a woman it was hard to do business with. However, in her time as Prime Minister the UK did sign up to the Single European Act and the Anglo-Irish agreement as well as the agreement to build the Channel Tunnel (McCormick, 2002 p.74). Margaret Thatcher was also one of the first Western leaders to believe that relations with the Soviet Union could improve, once Mikhail Gorbachev took power and let President Reagan know that. Her foreign policies certainly caused controversy; for instance, Margaret Thatcher alienated other Commonwealth governments by refusing to impose economic sanctions against South Africa. Groups opposed to the Apartheid regime certainly tried their own form of Public Diplomacy by urging the general public not to buy goods from South Africa. Disagreements over South Africa led to other Commonwealth governments imposing their own sanctions and even boycotting the Commonwealth Games held in Edinburgh in 1986. Margaret Thatcher was unrepentant that the UK completely disagreed with the rest of the Commonwealth (Comfort, 1993 p.305). Margaret Thatcher was not the first British Prime Minister to offer tacit support to the South African government by blocking anti-apartheid measures. The UK actually blocked proposed UN economic sanctions against South Africa and the other whites only regime of Southern Rhodesia over twenty times between 1965 and 1990 without much adverse publicity. Indeed, UK governments have successfully used Public Diplomacy techniques to portray themselves as being supportive of the UN. Public Diplomacy therefore cannot ensure that everybody supports government foreign policy, although it can most of the public apathetic at worst and supportive at best of such policy (Curtis, 2004).

It was to be the UK's relationship with the EEC that contributed to Margaret Thatcher's fall from power, and showed that relying on media support to promote the government's domestic and foreign policies is not always guaranteed to be successful. For many in the Conservative Party the signing of the Single European Act was as far as British involvement in the EEC should progress, as that would deliver the common market that they wanted. Thatcher was only concerned with liberalising international trade, and did not want to concede any more sovereignty to Brussels (Smith, 2003 p.230). She was not interested in deepening the European integration process as France, Germany, and then commission president Jacques Delores had wanted to do. Margaret Thatcher's determination to keep Britain out of unwanted integration was clearly put forward in her speech at Bruges (Gowland & Turner, 2000 p. 185). The agenda for further political integration beyond the economic co-operation had been implied in the Treaty of Rome, yet only advocated strongly with the poor economic performance of the 1970s. The UK was publicly the nation least favourable to closer political integration. Margaret Thatcher was the most vocal opponent of such plans (Bromley, Mackintosh, Brown, and Wuyts, 2004 p.16). At first glance her stance did not seem to be a risk to her position. Much of the press seemed to support her. Tabloid newspaper 'The Sun' went as far as using the headline 'up yours Delores!' Thatcher did not want to take Britain in the Exchange Rate Mechanism, which was the initial stage towards the single currency. Foreign Secretary Geoffrey Howe and Chancellor Nigel Lawson were in favour of

British entry, in the short term to lower interest rates, in the longer term to get Britain more closely integrated with the rest of Europe. Nigel Lawson and Geoffrey Howe both resigned in quick succession of each other, both men were replaced by the relatively unknown John Major. Europe was at this point dividing the Conservative Party to the point of being well publicised and very damaging to its electability. On the domestic front Thatcher's reputation was tarnished by the poll tax. John Major became Prime Minister as he convinced Thatcher loyalist supporters that he would continue her policies towards Europe, whilst telling the moderates he would change domestic policies. John Major delivered a surprise fourth consecutive Conservative election victory in 1992. Doing away with the poll tax and joining the ERM and also attacking Labour's tax and defence plans were the key to that success, with a helping hand from Labour's over confidence. Major had also briefly patched up Conservative divisions over Europe. However in reality the Major government was in a weakened domestic and international position. The government operated with a much smaller majority, which meant that divisions over Europe weakened it further. Internationally there was a global recession that badly affected the British economy, whilst other members of the EU were determined to deepen integration further. Major had to balance these factors and publicly present the government as being able to solve its problems (James, 2003 p.359).

The troubles of the Major government

After the 1992 general election things went from bad to disastrous for the Major government. Major was faced with having to negotiate in EU summits over the next steps in the integration process. He did not want to take Britain into a single currency, yet he did not want Britain to lose any influence in the EU. In the Maastricht Treaty, Major largely succeeded in his aims. The UK kept its opt out on the social charter and gained a further opt out of the single currency (McCormick, 2002 p.50). British opt outs were put forward as part of the concept of subisdiarity, that where possible decisions were devolved to the lowest tier of governance (McCormick, 2002 p.118). Major used Public Diplomacy to convince the British public that he had got he wanted. Although John Major could have been content with his diplomatic achievements at Maastricht, the defiance of Thatcherite backbenchers in opposing its ratification did untold political damage to his government's credibility (Young, 2003, p. 106). The Major government believed that opting out of the single currency was sensible, as it would not be popular with the electorate, and it was against the principles of the Conservative Party. Finally, the UK did not have to set high interest rates to maintain sterling at a fixed rate to meet convergence criteria if it did not want to. Major had the option to leave the ERM if he chose to. However, the UK withdrawal from the ERM was forced rather than voluntary, which is why it caused such harm to the Major government. Withdrawal from the ERM did assist British economic recovery but it still took a while for unemployment to start to decrease. Perhaps the most damaging impact for the Major government was that it lost crucial media support and had a reduced ability to promote and defend its policies to the British public. An unforeseen consequence for the conduct of Public Diplomacy that the problems of the Major government prompted would be New Labour's obsession with manipulating and managing media coverage (Hancock et al, 1998 p. 142). The Major government resisted moves towards a common foreign policy, which it considered impractical and undesirable, as well as being a further threat to British sovereignty. Given the scepticism of the British public towards such plans that opposition to them was one of the government's more popular diplomatic positions (Nugent, 2003 p.19).

John Major's initial talk of putting the UK at the heart of Europe was changed to a more sceptical approach once the UK was forced out of the ERM. The Conservative Party had staked its economic and foreign policies around staying in the ERM, yet unprecedented levels of currency speculation forced devaluation of the pound and therefore Britain's exit from the ERM. Aside from the embarrassment of having policy forced upon it the Major government believed that other EU members, France and Germany in particular did not help the UK resist the currency devaluation (Nicholson, 2002 p. 36). Inadvertently devaluation helped the British economy out of recession. The downside for the government was that it ruined its domestic creditability and harmed its reputation with its EU partners. Domestically, the events of Black Monday ruined the chances of the Conservatives being re-elected again. Within the EU the UK still retained the reputation of being a member state that obstructed progress (Nugent, 2003 p.19).

The UK was keen on allowing the former Warsaw Pact countries of Central and Eastern Europe to join the EU, as a means of driving forward their transitions towards liberal democracy (with the benefit of delaying the deepening of the integration process). The UK was in favour of the states of Central and Eastern Europe joining NATO, which the Czech Republic, Poland, and Hungary had done by the end of the 1990s (James, 2003 p. 392). Major was less keen on the development of common foreign and defence policies within the EU framework, although the inability of European governments to come up with effective strategies to solve the complex situations in the Former Yugoslavia demonstrated that was a long way from happening. The Major government came under pressure to intervene more decisively to protect civilians in Bosnia-Herzegovina (Ullman, 1996 p.81). Humanitarian agencies, human rights groups, Islamic groups and ordinary people appalled by events all wished to see Britain involved in peace enforcement, rather than ineffective peace keeping. Public sympathy was strongly supportive of helping Bosnian Muslims, especially when details of ethnic cleansing were widely reported. The war in Bosnia-Herzegovina was brought to an end when an American led NATO bombing campaign persuaded the Bosnian Serbs to stop fighting. The NATO campaign had received UN endorsement, a tacit acknowledgement that the UN, the EU, and individual states had been unable to end the conflict (Brown, 2002 p.144). The conflicts in the former Yugoslavia showed that the New World Order that President Bush had predicted in the wake of the collapse of communism in 1989 was not going to be as peaceful as some predicted. Conflicts such as those in Somalia, Sierra Leone, and Rwanda were all civil wars that started through the weakness of the respective national governments and their inability to control diverse internal forces. The instability of many African States dates back to the colonial period when state boundaries were drawn up by the colonial powers, without any consideration to tribal and ethnic divisions. Weak or corrupt post-colonial governments have found it hard to contain conflict caused by tribal divisions (Stott & Sullivan, 2000 p.259). The New World Order meant that things were in some respects less certain, whilst only the United States had the power to act alone in military terms. However, the increasing complexity of international relations means that the most effective diplomacy occurs when states act in unison, and some would suggest when they make decisions behind closed doors. Of course the spread of information technology and digital media coverage means that there can be greater public scrutiny of such decisions, and possibly greater public demand to alter or reverse those decisions. The greater scope of media coverage means that governments believe that they need to make a greater interest in managing the media presentation of their decisions. A fundamental weakness of the Major government was that it did not pay enough attention to the public presentation of its policies, whilst New Labour could be accused of putting spin ahead of sound policy decisions (James, 2003 p.443).

New Labour – New Diplomacy?

When the New Labour government was elected in 1997 the new Foreign Secretary Robin Cook promised a new more ethically based foreign policy and a more transparent Britain. He did not mean that every decision would be made upon an entirely ethical basis, although diplomacy would not be as cynically conducted as some suggested the Conservatives had done or indeed previous Labour governments had done (Higgins, June 2000). Previous Labour governments did not have such a good reputation for carrying out foreign policy as the Conservative governments had. New Labour had the distinct advantage of following in the wake of the Major administration that publicly appeared to have run out of ideas. The out going Major government was divided over Europe, and tarnished by allegations of sleaze, not even a healthy economy could save the Conservatives from electoral disaster. The New Labour government soon had a chance to prove its ethical credentials by supporting East Timor's moves towards regaining independence from Indonesia. A UN force eventually enforced independence, although it was Australia that led that UN force (Gott, 2005). Perhaps money and jobs had still come before ethics as New Labour had allowed the export of military aircraft to Indonesia, despite suspecting that those planes could have been used to bomb targets in East Timor. Governments especially if viewed through a realist perspective do not usually face clear diplomatic choices. Public Diplomacy was partly developed for the occasions when governments have to weigh up the domestic and foreign policy consequences of their decisions. Following ethically based policies could actually prove detrimental to narrowly defined national interests, whilst following national interests can sometimes lead to unethical decisions. Governments use Public Diplomacy to justify their decisions no matter how those decisions were made (MediaLens, 24 August 2005).

Perhaps not enough people in 1997 paid attention to the interest that Tony Blair had in foreign policy, or in his strong sense of patriotism, which like his other political, social, and economic views would have made him better suited to being in the Conservative Party. Tony Blair did not have much scope to decide or intervene in economic policy as Gordon Brown firmly controls the Treasury. Robin Cook may have liked to think that the UK was following an ethical foreign policy, yet it was the Prime Minister's ideas about making the UK more important and influential internationally. That sense of mission has dictated the most radical change of course in British diplomacy than at any time since the end of the Second World War. Blair got his way when it came to influencing and deciding UK diplomacy and had replaced Robin Cook with Jack Straw by 2001. As Foreign Secretary, Jack Straw was more in tune with Blair's beliefs and opinions (Gott, 2005).

After East Timor the next test of British foreign policy and diplomacy revolved around the issue of the Serbian province of Kosovo. Kosovo remained part of Serbia, even though the majority of its population was Albanian Kosovans. These Kosovans wished eventually to become part of Albania, though the Serbian government was determined to hold on to the province (James, 2003 p.419). The future of the province was by international law an internal Serbian matter, meaning that intervention should not have been expected or even be legal. The New Labour government was urged by some groups to intervene in Kosovo to stop the Serbians killing or expelling the whole Kosovan Albanian population.

Kosovan representatives also called for NATO intervention to protect them, yet also to allow autonomy or independence from Serbia. The UK and the Americans once again took the lead in the subsequent bombing campaign. The Serbians resisted NATO for longer than was expected, with the alliance switching from just attacking military targets in the province to bombing the Serbian capital Belgrade, and infrastructures such as power stations and bridges. The NATO campaign in Kosovo was unprecedented in international relations and diplomatic terms. Firstly, NATO had intervened in the internal affairs of a country that it had not been at war with. Secondly, the alliance justified its bombing of the rest of Serbia as a preventative measure that saved more lives in the long term, compared to the lives of those that died in the bombing. For Tony Blair the war in Kosovo firmly instilled the belief that war could be justified as a preventative war that in the long run protected lives. Certainly the New Labour government publicly insisted that the UK's involvement in the war was morally the best thing to have done. Tony Blair argued that moral values and humanitarian considerations motivated NATO involvement in the province, rather than thoughts of territorial or financial gain (Duffield, 2001 p. 41). Estimates of fatalities in Kosovo range from 10,000 to 30,000 Kosovans killed, with a further million leaving the province as refugees (Kessings, 1999 p.182).

The aims of New Labour's diplomacy and foreign policy were intended to change the world for better, although it soon found that the need to gain international agreement can water down the effectiveness of any actions to be taken. The incoming government had made commitments to increase aid to developing countries particularly those in Africa; it also wanted to increase international efforts to protect the environment to reduce the affects of global warming. New Labour gained power with the intention of building a peaceful, economically more prosperous, and politically more democratic Africa. Africa was chosen to receive more development aid as it was economically, politically, and environmentally in greater need of help than any other continent. The debt burden and combating the Aids pandemic were seen as the main areas in which Britain could help. As a means of getting the UK's Public Diplomacy widely known in the outside world it was highly effective. However, actual progress for the African states that needed help was delivered slowly (Abrahamsen & Williams, 2001 p. 249).

New Labour came to power with intentions of regenerating the UK politically, culturally, and economically through domestic economic reforms combined with attempts to rearrange British Public Diplomacy. The incoming government believed that too many people abroad had unfavourable views of the UK that were inaccurate and damaging its commercial and political prospects. Therefore, New Labour took steps to amend the UK's external image in order to correct conceptions that Britain was behind the times, a country in terminal decline and was not a place for foreigners, especially non-whites to visit due to racism and xenophobia. Although these initiatives were jokingly referred to as 'Cool Britannia' by the media, it was a serious attempt to re-brand Britain's image. The intention was to make the UK a more attractive place to visit, trade with, work in, and even move to (Leonard, Small, & Rose, 2005 p.2). The Cool Britannia schemes were run by non-governmental organisations such as the British Council and the British Tourist Authority, rather than the government itself. The New Labour government believed that the £800 million spent annually by the Foreign and Commonwealth Office was money well spent (Leonard, Small, & Rose, 2005 p.3).

Chapter 4

<u>Diplomacy before 9/11</u>

New Labour as a governing party has probably been the government most obsessed with managing its media image and presenting its side of every story as quickly as possible, which may be incompatible with its intentions to have ethically based foreign policy. Margaret Thatcher had been keeping her press officers busy and ensuring that her government appeared to be in control of every situation. Labour had not shown such astuteness in handling the media to its advantage. Therefore, New Labour's obsession with handling and controlling the media dates back to the Labour Party's long period in opposition. The Conservatives were used to the majority of the press supporting them and did not have a similar obsession for manipulating the media. Tony Blair was a man that became Prime Minister determined to ensure that the media always represented him as being in control, being decisive, and being a man that that was capable of running the UK efficiently. From the start New Labour wished to portray itself as being in charge of the country. New Labour's handling of the media was sleek; the government's reaction to events was fast and effective. In other words, New Labour was well aware of the techniques by which it could use Public Diplomacy to its best advantage. The war in Kosovo had demonstrated that government press officers and media consultants or spin-doctors as they are frequently referred to, could find a means to present the UK's foreign policy in the most favourable perspective. In this respect, the chief spin-doctor Alastair Campbell was showing his great value to the government. The Kosovo war proved that Tony Blair and the American President Bill Clinton had a strong working relationship that helped Anglo-American relations (Naughtie, 2004 p. 55). Both men were more than willing to intervene in an international crisis; both were intent to justify their actions publicly through the media. President Clinton was also aware that New Labour was ready to support any action against Saddam Hussein's regime in Iraq if action was required. For instance, the UK joined in the air strikes and missile attacks on Iraq in 1998. Public Diplomacy was key to trying to maintain diplomatic pressure on Iraq, although its regime was not deterred by harsh economic sanctions or limited missile strikes. It became apparent that there two ways of solving the impasse over Iraq, either slowly through UN sanctions and weapons inspections; or by direct military intervention led by the Americans whether approved or not by the UN. The consequences of 9/11 would change how Public Diplomacy worked and have consequences on the conduct of international relations (Hirsh, 2003 p.3)

<u>The affects of 9/11</u>

Tony Blair was initially unsure of his relationship with George W. Bush once he started his presidency. President Bush was widely regarded as more of an isolationist than Clinton who had taken a great interest in foreign policy in the wake of the collapse of communism was. However, events took a course that few managed to predict, and which meant that the emphasis on the UK's diplomacy would shift dramatically. The catalyst for these changes was the 9/11 attacks on New York and Washington carried out by Al-Qaeda operatives after they hijacked American airliners and crashed them into the World Trade Center and the Pentagon (Baxter & Downing, 2001 p.3). The UK government offered help immediately, and has arguably worked more closely with the American government than anytime since the Second World War. Once the American government could prove that the 9/11 attacks were carried out by Al-Qaeda, President Bush announced the war on terror (Hirsh, 2003 p.3). The way in which both countries have conducted the war on terror has caused a great deal of debate and controversy. It has brought the way in which British governments conduct diplomacy into focus. The first stage of the war on terror was relatively easy to justify, and that was the removal of the Taliban regime in Afghanistan. The Taliban had seized power in Afghanistan amidst the chaos and in fighting that typified the country following the withdrawal of Soviet forces in 1989. The Taliban had allowed Osama Bin-laden and Al-Qaeda to use Afghanistan as a base for its operations. Al-Qaeda in return offered assistance in the civil war against the Northern Alliance. The Taliban and Al-Qaeda also had strong links with Pakistan's secret services that dated back to the resistance of the Soviet invasion

during the 1980s. The Pakistani government soon offered to support
the American government in return for military and financial
assistance (Ahmed, 2005 p. 145). The American led invasion of
Afghanistan quickly defeated and removed the Taliban without
destroying it as a fighting force. The defeat of the Taliban affected
Al-Qaeda, yet it did not destroy it. Bin-Laden was not caught or
captured or killed as had been hoped. Whilst Bin-Laden has
survived, Al-Qaeda has shown its endurance and flexibility which
means that the war on terror is a long way from been won. The
United States and the UK seem to have miscalculated when it comes
to the determination of Al-Qaeda to continue the struggle with no
intentions of giving up. The campaigns against Al-Qaeda have led
to the use of Public Diplomacy to justify the tactics employed by the
Americans and the British. The UK government has noticeably
backed the United States through most of the diplomatic arguments
and events since 9/11. Even more than during the Cold War the UK
government is attempting to justify all the means used in the war on
terror with the overriding aim of defeating Al-Qaeda (Halliday, 2002
p. 20).

The war on Iraq

It has been the use of Public Diplomacy by New Labour to justify
action against Iraq that proved very controversial (Curtis, 2004).
There were claims that Saddam Hussein had ordered the production
of weapons of mass destruction (WMD), which was why he was
unwilling to co-operate fully with UN weapons inspectors. The Iraqi
regime also had an appalling human rights record, most notably the
suppression of the Shiite and Kurdish rebellions in the immediate
wake of the Gulf War. The British government used Public
Diplomacy to gather international support for an invasion of Iraq and
limit domestic opposition. Tony Blair emphasised the immediate
threat that Iraqi WMD posed to countries in the Middle East,
especially Israel, Kuwait and Saudi Arabia. Bush was following the
usual American policy of protecting Middle East oil supplies
(Parker, 1998, p.172, Gott, 2005). Britain and the United States
attempted to gather international support by using Public Diplomacy
and the use of intelligence and information (some would suggest
disinformation). Statements were made emphasising Iraq's appalling

human rights record as well as the threat of WMD, whilst portraying the morality of the UK's position. For instance, Jack Straw frequently stated that British foreign policy would be most effective when regimes that abused human rights were stood up to, persuaded to change their ways, or as a last resort removed from power. The gist of his argument was that Saddam Hussein should be removed, as he would change his regime (The Guardian, Tuesday March 26 2002). The human rights approach did not seem to gain enough support and was therefore only a secondary argument behind the WMD claims. One intelligence dossier quoted by Tony Blair stated that Iraq could launch such weapons within 45 minutes. These claims were made with the objectives of shoring up domestic support for military action and attempting to get a UN resolution that sanctioned an invasion of Iraq. Domestically, claims about WMD meant that action against Iraq was not unpopular with a majority of the public. There were those that were opposed to the war from the onset on moral as well as upon legal ground (The Guardian, Monday March 15 2004). As a means to gain support for a second UN resolution it was a dismal failure. As the resolution was going to be vetoed by France and possibly Russia and China it was dropped. Tony Blair had wanted UN backing to legitimise military action and to reduce domestic and foreign opposition (Naughtie, 2004, p.126). Critics of the Anglo-American plans to invade Iraq pointed out that the Iraqi regime probably did not have any WMD left after the Gulf War and that such accusations were made to cover up the settling of old scores. America's main motive was greed; it was only interested in controlling Iraqi oil supplies. Whilst Tony Blair based the UK's decision to act against Iraq upon his moral vision for the world, the methods used to achieve that vision are ironically enough lacking in morality and are legally problematic. In many respects New Labour was unable to effectively use Public Diplomacy to justify the war in Iraq because the British public was becoming increasingly sceptical about the truthfulness of its spin and media or press releases. The British media has not always shown willingness to present press releases without criticising their contents (The Guardian, Monday March 15 2004).

In purely military terms the invasion of Iraq was a success, the Iraqi's were no match for the better-equipped coalition forces. In political and diplomatic terms the invasion was far from successful. Claims about Iraqi WMD were never substantiated by any evidence that such weapons had existed (Dean, 2004, p.199). Given the military inferiority of his forces, Saddam Hussein would have probably ordered the use of such weapons. The failure to find any WMD in Iraq brought into doubt either the expertise of British intelligence or the honesty of the government, or both. Revelations that the government played up the danger that Iraq posed made British involvement less popular with the public and affected the popularity of Tony Blair himself. Things were made worse for the government when the BBC reporter Nick Gillingham alleged that the dossier used to claim Iraq could use WMD in 45 minutes had been 'sexed up'. It was rumoured that the BBC had been given information by the Ministry of Defence expert David Kelly who later committed suicide (ePolitix.com). Allegations and counter-allegations between the government and the BBC eventually led to the resignations of senior BBC figures. The government called for the Hutton enquiry to investigate the affair (Young, 2003 p.311). The findings of the enquiry were claimed to be a white wash by the critics when the government was cleared of any wrongdoing. Certainly, it must be assumed that Tony Blair and Jack Straw must have known there was little chance of WMD being found let alone being used. It is yet another instance of a British government misleading the general public with Public Diplomacy. In opposition New Labour had complained about the amoral and cynical diplomacy of the Thatcher and Major governments, yet in office New Labour has proved adept at using cynical diplomacy and media disinformation in the pursuit of its objectives. However not everybody is fooled or persuaded by it's arguments (MediaLens, 24 August 2005).

Although the Iraqi regime had been overthrown, the UK and the United States found it very difficult to establish peace and stability in Iraq. Under Saddam Hussein, Islamic militants such as Al-Qaeda had no influence in Iraq, despite anything that President Bush suggested prior to the American led invasion. The removal of Saddam Hussein allowed such groups to operate freely. The presence of American and British troops provided Al-Qaeda with thousands of potential targets and the chance to recruit new members in Iraq. However, it has been ordinary Iraqi citizens that have suffered most from ambushes and suicide bombs. It seems that Tony Blair and President Bush spent so much time and effort in the diplomatic and military preparations that they paid no consideration to what to do in Iraq once Saddam Hussein was ousted. The internal situation in Iraq was and remains more complicated than the British and United States governments had counted upon. This has proved to be a miscalculation that has had more poor consequences for Tony Blair's domestic and external reputation. The instability in Iraq has led to the public questioning why British troops should remain there when their presence seems to be achieving little and puts their lives at risk. In terms of diplomacy, the involvement in Iraq has meant that the UK has maintained its closer relationship with the United States, whilst damaging its relationships with France and Germany, as well as other critics of the Iraq war. Initial efforts of justifying intervention were only partially successful in gaining public support. The failure to gain UN backing damaged the chances of the war having widespread international support. Tony Blair certainly believed that the intervention was indeed needed to make the world a better place. However, the situation in Iraq contributed to New Labour's unpopularity and its reduced majority after the 2005 election (Gott, 2005).

The government made concerted efforts to gain positive media coverage of its actions and policies, although British television in general and the BBC in particular was prepared to be critical of what the government did. President Bush did not have the same problem, as a whole the American media had not been prepared to criticise foreign policy decisions since 9/11, although academics and a few celebrities have attempted to condemn America's actions. In the aftermath of events in Iraq there has been plenty of debate in the United States about what the United States needs to do next in its foreign policy, particularly since its present strategy in Iraq is deemed to failed. Despite the unpopularity of involvement in Iraq, the level of debate over the UK's future foreign policy and diplomacy is much less noticeable (Leonard, Small, & Rose, 2005 p.1).

New Labour's Public Diplomacy after 9/11 has led its critics to accuse it of cynicism, amorality, and even illegality. Although the idealist foreign policy alleged to have been the aim of Robin Cook was never going to become reality, New Labour's foreign policy has like its domestic policy disappointed those that are politically left of centre (MediaLens, 24 august 2005). The tactics adopted as part of the war on terror have alienated many British Muslims, and was part of the motivation behind the 7/7 attacks on London in 2005. Muslims have also been alarmed by the security measures introduced as part of the UK's internal anti-terrorist policy, for instance increased numbers of stop and search carried out on Muslim men. The attacks on London were an attempt to stop the UK government's support for the American war on terror (The Mirror, 9 July 2005). However it remains unlikely that the UK would stop supporting the Americans in the war on terror whether New Labour continues in government or if the Conservatives regained power. As the British support for American moves to stop the nuclear programmes of Iran and North Korea demonstrate that support could lead to further conflict, with further usage of Public Diplomacy to vindicate such conflict (Leonard, Small, & Rose, 2005 p.1).

Concluding Remarks

Therefore, it could be argued that Public Diplomacy has had and does have an impact upon the conduct of the UK's diplomacy and foreign policy. The role and influence that Public Diplomacy has on the formulation, and thus upon the exercise of British foreign policy can be argued to be variable, depending on circumstances, and the influence of different individuals, groups, and organisations within and from outside the UK government. The primary function of Public Diplomacy is to communicate information and government opinion to foreign audiences whilst having an eye out for influencing public opinion in the UK. Traditional behind closed doors form of diplomacy were regarded, and to a great extent are still regarded as the most effective ways to enhance or at least maintain the position of any state within the international system. Diplomacy put simply is the means by which nation states have full sovereignty over their internal territory, and that these nation states have power and influence in their relationships with other nation states. The concept of sovereignty in theory allows nation states to conduct their diplomacy and foreign policy without any actual constraints in their attempts to fully promote their national interests. Political, economic, cultural, and technological changes or developments have meant that there are practical and theoretical constraints of traditional diplomacy and national sovereignty. The adoption of Public Diplomacy, or at least some of its elements, is both a cause and a reflection of those political, economic, cultural, and technological developments, which when together as a whole are usually termed to be the process of globalisation. Globalisation has meant paradoxically that there are challenges to national sovereignty that can coincide with other factors that can strengthen sovereignty instead. It is improved technology that has allowed national governments to use Public Diplomacy to effectively communicate their ideas, and details of actual or proposed policy actions to ever-greater levels of internal and external audiences. The media, and non-governmental organisations to describe, assess, and sometimes to criticise the policies of the UK government has also used technological changes. Governments in Western Democracies theoretically and in practice do not have to change internal and external policies or their diplomacy, due to criticisms from the media and non-governmental organisations. Although governments could consider changes to the public presentation of their foreign policy, even if they do not change actual policy or their actual diplomatic approach to various issues.

The objectives of UK foreign policy and diplomacy have been remarkably consistent over the last few decades. The main objectives have been national security, the promotion of trade, protecting trade, the UK's trading links, and maintaining an international balance of power. Public Diplomacy has been regarded as a means to achieve such objectives, as well as being a method to hide any undesirable consequences of British diplomacy. The UK's decline since its industrial, economic, and naval supremacy peaks during the 19th century has meant that foreign policy and diplomacy have had to be amended accordingly to achieve the country's objectives. The financial, military, and political impacts of the First and Second World Wars drastically reshaped the circumstances that British diplomacy operated in. As British power has declined so the need for multilateral solutions to diplomatic and political issues has increased. Therefore, UK governments have often been good at assessing changes to the country's economic, political, and military situation circumstances even if their diplomacy has occasionally lagged behind. By and large traditional diplomacy allowed the UK to be on the winning sides in both world wars, although it be could argued that a lack of nerve, and an even greater lack of resources meant that inter-war British diplomacy did not prevent further conflict. The UK government in the immediate post-war period also used traditional diplomatic methods when the need for continued links with the United States, and the need for stronger ties with the rest of Western Europe was quickly recognised. The UK also had to deal with its weakened international position through the continuation of the transatlantic alliance, and by commencing the de-colonisation process. UK governments were slower to work closely with the rest of Western Europe, and kept out of the first stages of European integration.

It was the conditions caused by and reflected in the Cold War that helped to formally introduce Public Diplomacy into the conduct of British foreign policy. Non-governmental organisations started to have more influence on the UK, the UN and NATO for instance. These organisations did not take away national sovereignty from the UK, yet they helped to alter the perceptions of British governments in relation to international relations. The onset of the Cold War meant that Britain was involved in the ideological as well as the military and political rivalry of the superpowers as an ally of the United States. A permanent seat on the UN Security Council and the acquisition of nuclear weapons meant that the UK was still a great power, even if it could not match the might of the superpowers. The American government developed Public Diplomacy during the Cold War to justify some of its more morally dubious foreign policy decisions in its attempts to prevent the global spread of communism. The UK used some dubious methods of its own in its attempts to delay the independence of Kenya and Malaya until suitable post-colonial governments were put into place. The UK was not so heavily involved in the fight against communism outside of Western Europe once the remaining vestiges of the British Empire was extinguished. Public Diplomacy has served the role of justifying the UK's role in military conflicts. Examples of this role include the public support for the Falklands War and its acceptance that three Gulf War of 1990-91 had to be fought to liberate Kuwait. Public Diplomacy was also used in the same role to gain public support for the invasion of Iraq with less successful results.

In many ways it was the issues surrounding whether or not the UK should join the EEC as it then was that gave Public Diplomacy more influence in the diplomacy of the UK governments. British governments sought to increase the general public's support for British entry during the 1960s. Both Conservative and Labour governments found it was impossible to persuade General de Gaulle that the UK should join, convincing the British public that British membership was a good thing was relatively easy in comparison. Edward Heath took the UK into the EEC, despite strong public and parliamentary opposition. When the Wilson government took power in 1974 it promised to re-negotiate the British terms of entry; it also held a referendum on continued membership of the EEC. Membership of the EU has certainly brought constitutional, political, and diplomatic dilemmas for UK governments. Arguably, the processes of the EU work best behind closed doors. As the EU has become more important national governments have used Public Diplomacy as a means to put forward their objectives. UK governments certainly believe the role of Public Diplomacy is useful in publicly putting across its main objectives before key summit meetings and treaty negotiations. The public announcement of what British governments hope to achieve or prevent is a risky strategy, as it could backfire if the government gets nothing that it wants. Sometimes it is best for British governments to negotiate through traditional diplomacy and then make public the results of the agreements reached. Both Labour and Conservative governments have found it difficult to balance the desire to remain within the EU without deepening British involvement in the integration process. New Labour has so far not held a promised referendum on the UK joining the single currency, as all public opinion polls suggest that the electorate would vote against it. Membership of the EU has meant Britain has had to share sovereignty which could be taken back it was decided to leave the EU.

Public Diplomacy also relates to cultural and educational links to other countries. The processes of globalisation, European integration, and immigration have enhanced such links. The growth of information technology, and worldwide travel opportunities has made the world a smaller place. These changes have also meant that UK governments feel the need to promote such links as well as trying to promote the national interest. The UK has developed a concern for aiding developing countries and protecting the environment. This approach is commendable although often the reality has not lived up to the hype.

The 2016 vote in favour of the UK leaving the EU surprised many and it's consequences could be felt decades into the future.

Bibliography

Abercrombie N, Hill S & Turner B S, (2000) The Penguin Dictionary of Sociology 4th edition, Penguin Group, London

Abrahamsen R, & Williams P, (2001) Ethical Foreign Policy: the Antinomies of New Labour's Third Way in Sub-Saharan Africa, Political Studies: 2001, Vol. 49

Ahmed N M, (2005) The war on truth – 9/11, disinformation, and the anatomy of terrorism, Arris, Gloucestershire

Baldwin D A, (1985) Economic Statecraft, Princeton University Press, Princeton

Bark D L, & Gress D R, (1993) A History of West Germany – From shadow to substance 1945-1963, Blackwell, Oxford

Barton R P, (1997) Modern Diplomacy, Longman, London and New York

Baxter J & Downing M, (2001) The Day That Shook The World Understanding September 11th, BBC News, London

Benn, (1988) Office without Power, Dairies 1968-72, Arrow Books Limited, London

Brendon P, the Dark Valley – A Panorama of the 1930s (2000) Jonathan Cape, London

Bromley, Mackintosh, Brown, and Wuyts (2004) - Making the International: Economic Interdependence and Political Order, Pluto Press, London

Brown C, (2001) Understanding International Relations 2nd edition, Palgrave, Basingstoke

Brown C, with Ainley K, (2005) Understanding International Relations 3rd edition, Palgrave, Basingstoke

Bullock A, (1983) Ernest Bevin: Foreign Secretary 1945-1951, Norton, New York

Chossudovsky M, - War Propaganda, Spectre Magazine 3 February 2003

Comfort N (1993) Brewer's Politics, a phrase and fable dictionary, Cassell, London

Coxall B, Robins L & Leach R (2003) Contemporary British Politics 4th edition, Palgrave, London

Curtis M, Britain's real foreign policy and the failure of British academia, International Relations, Vol.18, No.3, September 2004

Dean, J W, (2004) Worse than Watergate - the secret Presidency of George W. Bush, Little, Brown and Company, London

Dickie J, (1994) Special No More, Anglo-American Relations: Rhetoric and Reality, Weidenfeld & Nicholson, London

Djerejian Report (2003) "Changing Minds Winning Peace: A New Strategic Direction for U.S. Public Diplomacy in the Arab & Muslim World,"

Hancock M D, Conradt D P, Guy Peters B, Safran W, and Zariski R, (1998) Politics in Western Europe – second edition, Macmillan Press, Basingstoke

Duffield M, (2001) Global Governance and the New Wars, Zed Books, London and New York

Dunbabin J P D (1994) The Cold War – The Great Powers and their allies, Longman, London

Epolitix.com - Bea Campbell Interview with Clare Short MP about Labour Foreign Policy, Iraq and the Hutton Enquiry

Eatwell & Wright (2003) Contemporary Political Ideologies 2nd Edition, Continuum, London

Evans & Newnham, (1998) The Penguin Dictionary of International Relations, Penguin, London

Fielding-Smith A, The damage done, The Guardian, Monday March 15, 2004

Friedman T, (2003) Longitudes and Attitudes – Exploring the World before and after September 11, Penguin, London

Gott, (2005) The Third Crusade, New Left Review 33, May-June 2005

Gowland D, & Turner A, (2000) Britain and European Integration – A Documentary History, Routledge, London and New York

Greenwood S, (2000) Britain and the Cold War 1945-91, Macmillan Press Ltd, Basingstoke

Halliday F, (2002) Two Hours That Shook the World, Saqi Books, London

Higgins J- Saintly or Cynical: An Ethical Dimension to Foreign Policy? ISIS Briefing Paper No. 77, June 2000

Hirsh (2003), M. At War with Ourselves – Why America is squandering its chance to build a better world, Oxford University Press, Oxford

Hobsbawm E, (1962) The Age of Revolution 1789-1848,

Weidenfeld & Nicholson, London

Hobsbawm, E (1994) Age of Extremes, the Short Twentieth Century 1914-1991, Michael Joseph, London

Horne A, (1989) Harold Macmillan II: 1957-1986, Penguin, London

Hurd D, (1997) The Search for Peace A Century of Peace Diplomacy, Little Brown and Company, London

James, H (2003) Europe Reborn – A History, 1914 – 2000, Pearson Longman, Harlow

Johnston I and McAuley R (2000) The Battleships, 4 Books, London

Kennedy P (1976) The Rise and fall of British Naval Mastery, Penguin, London

Kerr P, (1990) The Penguin Book of Lies, Viking, London

Kessings, (December 1999) Yugoslavia Report, from N M Naimark, Fires of Hatred: Ethnic cleansing in Twentieth century Europe, Harvard University Press, Cambridge

Kissinger H, (1994) Diplomacy, Simon & Schuster, New York and London

Leonard M, Small A, & Rose M, (2005) British Public Diplomacy in the Age of Schisms, Counterpoint, The Foreign Policy Centre, London

Madgwick P, (1994) A new introduction to British Politics, Stanley Thornes, Cheltenham

McCormick, (2002) - Understanding the European Union, Palgrave, London

MediaLens - The Dark Heart of Robin Cook's 'Ethical' Foreign Policy - Part 2, 24 August 2005

Middlemas K, (1972) Diplomacy of Illusion

Mirror.co.uk, SO WHAT DO THEY WANT? Mirror 9 July 2005

Morgan K O, (1993) The Oxford Popular History of Britain, Oxford University Press, Oxford

Morgenthau H J, (1993) Politics Among Nations – the struggle for power and peace (brief edition) McGraw-Hill Inc, New York

Naughtie J, (2004) The Accidental American, Tony Blair and the Presidency, Macmillan, London

Nicholson M, International Relations – A concise introduction 2nd edition, Palgrave, Basingstoke

Norton-Taylor R, Straw signals decisive new era for foreign policy, The Guardian, Tuesday March 26, 2002

Nugent N, (2003) The Government and Politics of the European Union 5th edition, Palgrave, London

Oxford English Reference Dictionary, (1996). Oxford University Press, Oxford

Resources for the Study of International Relations and Foreign Policy website: http://hpol.org/churchill/

Parker G, (1998) Geopolitics – Past, Present and Future, Pinter, London

Roberts J.M, (1996) A History of Europe, Penguin, London

Ryan D, (2003) The United States and Europe in the Twentieth Century, Pearson Longman, London and New York

Schama S, (2002) A History of Britain 3 – the End of Empire 1776-2000, BBC, London

Smith D, (2003) Free Lunch –Easily Digestible Economics, Served on a plate, Profile Books, London

Spiller J, Clancy T, Young S, and Mosley S (2005) - The United States 1763 – 2001 Routledge, London

Stafford D (1999) Roosevelt & Churchill – Men of Secrets, Little, Brown and Company, London

Stott P & Sullivan S (2000) Political Ecology - Science, Myth and Power, Arnold, London

Todd A, (2001) Democracies and Dictatorships – Europe and the World 1919 – 1989, Cambridge University Press, Cambridge

Ullman, (1996)

Ward G, (2003) The Rough Guide History of the USA, Rough Guides Ltd, London

Watson J, (1997) Success in World History since 1945, John Murray, London

Wikipedia – Public Diplomacy, from Wikipedia website

Young H, (2003) supping with the Devils – Political writing from Thatcher to Blair, Guardian Books, London

www.ingramcontent.com/pod-product-compliance
Lightning Source LLC
Chambersburg PA
CBHW051122250726
48655CB00007B/2840